VERSES FROM THE CENTRAL JAIL

VERSES FROM THE CENTRAL JAIL

Héctor de la O

Library of Congress Control Number: 2013907950
ISBN: 979-8-89465-018-0 (sc)
ISBN: 979-8-89465-019-7 (e)

Printed in the United States of America.

Integrity Publishing
39343 Harbor Hills Blvd Lady Lake, FL 32159

www.integrity-publishing.com

1.

Someone in the chambers of the Lord gave witness
Of His love to share with waifs without a home,
Come into my life to teach me of His goodness,
Offering safe harbor to a child, just a beaten dog,
Rare kindness, and his wife was like a grandmother.
Ramirez was his surname and his eponym Succor;
Of course he was repentant of this wild origins.

Ruddy as a Michoacán Tarasco and as solid
As a wrestler, a game cock always on his arm,
My nino was an honest man although he drank,
If not what kind of indio would he represent?
Reliable to bring the mercy of the Lord to El Sereno,
Every Saturday my heart would race his Chevrolet,
Zero to sixty in a heartbeat to Green Meadows.

Chabela would be waiting and I loved her also,
Hospitable and soft-spoken as Socorro was,
A stack of flour tortillas always freshly-made
Belied her southern birth near León or Moroleón;
Each one brought me joy and fed my soul to gratitude.
Light years away they live today until tomorrow,
And I hope the Lord forgives me for abandoning them.

H. d. l. O. – 14 FEB 06

Chabela was Isabel Gonzales, from Guanajuato, Mexico – She was
thirty years older than her husband, Socorro (They were really the
godparents of my younger brother, Xavier Santiago – "Nino", short
for "padrino" - Mexican slang for "godfather").

He was one of the old-school "sewer men" of Los Angles –
pick-and-shovel, clay pipe-laying plumbers, and I even worked
with him in the ditches as a teenager. Old Jack Stephan and
Adee (famous plumbers thereabout) probably still remember old
Socorro.

Once, he recounted, he was on a job in a ditch in the street and
had to go to the toiled – When he got back, there was a ruckus
going on at the ditch. Apparently a worker had gotten buried.
So he grabbed his shovel and jumped in, everyone frantically
shoveling to get their buddy out. So he asks this guy, "Hey, who's
buried down there?" and the guy tells him, "Some guy named
Socorro." So he answers him, "But I'm Socorro!" Needless to say
they were all relieved – But Socorro always laughed about that.

2.

Evening and morning and the blessed strung a lute;
Divinely even so were words of truth inspired.
Oh, and on the thirteenth day they gathered,
Unforeseen some others witnessing this interlude.
And in Heaven they performed their own civilities,
Round about the throne of the Almighty chanting
Dulcet accolades to Whom their gifts were owing.

In the meantime were those witnesses corrupted,
Vaunting blasphemies before the judge in the salons,
Envious of what they couldn't do and critical the more,
Secure in the respect they'd garnered over time,
Each of them renowned for speaking in an evil tone
Every time a valid inspiration graced a scene;
Now shall the shades of time exonerate your hand!

On the appointed day before the passing of the age,
Light years from the predetermination of all things,
Your calling like a laurel will reflect the spectrum –
Many have been called but few will be the chosen.
Put your hand into the muse's hand and walk
In wisdom – For the knowledge of your blessing in itself
Attests so eloquently to your talent and your grace

Héctor de la O
22 APR 05

Critics, cynics, dogs. Yours is a meretricious lot. What in the name of bloody Hell, and barkin' that you can describe the very soul of beauty!

Don't you sell your vacuous reviews to garner the acclaim
of other heartless, helpless reprobates? Such elevated taste
must needs be shared amongst your bedfellows!

Get ye hence! Go count the pimples on your damaged arses,
and desist from your supercilious expoundings on aesthetics.

Embittered by your lack of skill, your drivel in the dailies
and the rags is but the whimpering of empty-headed fools,
accompanied by those who buy into your self-uplifting
touted erudition.

Go float in the lake of fire surrounded by whomever would
subscribe to vitriol, to diatribe and blasphemy. See ya!
Wouldn't wanna be ya!

3.

Flit across the fields and brush away my tears,
Like a paper toy which fancies its own flight,
Utterly aimless, leaving color everywhere you go;
To the young you are a wispy bit if liberty,
Transcending the oppressive pull of gravity,
Earthbound long enough but to alight upon a petal.
Rivers passing the underneath erasing all frontiers,
Borne upon the wind as fleet as silent thought,
You conquer the expanse of space and time.

Butterfly, what name had you before a day in June,
Unidentified flying object before Adam ere the fall?
To the Japanese an unrequited love and suicide,
To heavyweights elusive flight and stinging blows;
Every flower knows your name in Saigon City,
Recluses in Guyana called you Papillion for years,
Finally forever free to Venezuela's arms and love,
Let your wingbeats echo through the Copper Canyon's walls,
Yonder take my secrets to Felicitas Sapién.

H. d. l, O – 11 JAN 06

Felicitas Sapién was my grandmother, very elegantly slim and tall
as was her sister Lupe (who dressed all in black after the death
of her husband, for the rest of her life). Both were so obviously
native – And because they were from Chihuahua, probably
Tarahumara. Naturally, racial stigma being what it is, they always
denied that heritage.

My grandfather Pedro Pichardo (My father always said we came
from the French), worked for the postal system of Chihuahua at
Hidalgo del Parral. During the Mexican Revolution of 1910,
Doroteo Arango Arámbula, a native of Durango and better known
by his nom de guerre, "Pancho Villa", always sought to murder him.
Pedro died anyway, failing out of a walnut tree into which he'd
climbed to shake the branches for some children below (That's the
story they told my father as a child). Pancho Villa (poetic justice!)
was assassinated in that very town of Hidalgo del Parral in 1923.

My family (of the Porras branch, mainly) of Camargo, hated Villa
for murdering more than thirty women, some with their children,
because one of the women insulted him.

After my grandfather died, Felicitas took her children north to
Ciudad Juárez, Chihuahua, and then across the border to El Paso.
My father, Santiago, was raised there and died and is buried there,
in the military cemetery at Fort Bliss. He was a veteran of WW II,
and fought at Normandy (Our ancestors, of the ancient family
name of Picard, came from Brittany originally – the province next to
Normandy)

4.

Gusto for the flesh of men,
And you're a bodhisattvah?
Youth elixirs shall not stay
Judicial retribution's pantheon,
Unless eternal life has varied
Avenues to reach the goal,
Novel strategies to no avail.

Pray the sun to wisdom wake,
Or shall your disregard for time
Lay bare the soul of apathy,
Arriving at contrived repentance,
Nowhere evident until too late?
Cosmic are the consequences
On the day the clock rings last.

H. d. l. O – 27 FEB 06

5.

Some people love and give and make mistakes and live;
Except for victims everyone enjoys the fruits of being here.
Right now you're driving past those trees around the bend;
Isn't that the place where No. 3 paid retribution for her kind?
At home you have her comb, her locket or her handkerchief,
Lying still as she, her fragrance clinging to the atmosphere.

Kindship elsewhere torn asunder clings to shreds of memory,
If only this if only that I wonder where she is so far away!
Life goes on and death awaits us all including lonely men,
Lepers never to be cleansed as also Esau wept for naught.
Every now and then you'll get the urge to roam about again,
Right up until the day the laws at least of physics claim you.

Never has a sanction so severe been served upon a vandal,
Over the objection of your dream team, learned scholars all.
When the final grains of sand comingle with the last few drops
Your I.V. unit sends into your veins your heart will race no more;
On the morrow shall you join your sacrifices in a common grave,
Until the day we rise and you are culled from the procession.

Did you think it was ignored, your interruption of their innocence?
If death was merciful to maidens bleeding in some forest glen,
Eternity will be their crown for wanton slaughters they endured,
Tomorrow shall the handiwork of the Almighty walk these avenues,
Oblivious of danger as Abaddon arrests your soul from wanderings;
On the reason for untimely death you had your time to ponder.

Héctor de la O – 03 MAR 06

6.

Just like when you were a little girl you steal the show,
Erupting onto the frenetic scene like Greta Garbo,
Such panache aplomb and chutzpah verve and moxie!
Savoir faire I wouldn't venture an opinion on for tastes
Invariably are the domain of every monkey on his vine;
Each one of us will swing to our very heart's delight.

Many years ago in 1924 Josefa, beauty of the Kora, gave
On your father's birthday what a perfect gift, a child,
Though someone to contend with as it now turns out,
Harboring the love of Heaven and the fire of Hell in one
Eternally determined woman child to be mother to three
Rebellious boys though now reformed and blessed still.

Of course some people talk about you as do you in turn,
Forever struggling with creation for the sake of pettiness.
May you see the light and sell Jack's house and end a play
In God's good time surrounded by other than the vultures.
No one lives forever in his mother's house but marries off,
Ending his own days as they began, beholden to a woman.

Héctor de la O – 09 MAR 06

No matter whom I talk to, no one can live with his mother – once he
or she is grown, except for derelicts, and then they come out in the
newspapers for throttling the old hag.

Others are these pretty little boys – Hear them talking in their backyard through the fence, about "Avocado facial cream" or some such nonsense.

So mothers, don't invite your sons over for fetid leftovers – If they say the way to a man's heart is through his stomach, for God's sake don't poison the poor bastard!

And stop wondering why your daughters-in-law won't take your crap. Let's live and let live. Your family would grow much bigger if your own people didn't run from you every time we see you. See you later, I'll come around once in a while.

7.

Back then it was the war in Viet Nam and Nixon held your post,
Undoing his undoing by the grace of loopholes built into the law,
So that politics allows for character assassination but by edict.
Hand in hand opposing parties make their beds and sleep alone.

Send in the Marines; the Jarheads never being schooled in civics,
Every time go marching off in rout step to defeat in others' lands,
Never yet a worthy foe of Mayan drunkards or under-aged cadets,
Delivered by the flipside of inevitable fate, manifest destiny undone.

To this day I still recall the musings of ignorant inner-city dwellers,
Handsome youths too young to waste but never to see home again,
Educated by the bullet that was meant for me but for mere mercy;
Many other never felt nor heard their own report but yards away.

Always suffering for the simple lack of the essential of a might nation,
While starving little dark-skinned people fighting to defend a home
Awaken us to realizations never meant for the unlearned and unclean;
Youth is wasted on the young but never truth on battle-weary men.

Today's fat cats on the other hand for the most part learned in class
How valuable deferments are, for who would send his son away to die?
If their birthright spared them from the horrors of the battlefield,
Selective service singles out the underprivileged for heroic deaths.

To our detriment we cross the skies and to the loss of our prestige,
In a time when lies usurp the truth and infidels abound to judge
Misplaced affinities – Visions of an everlasting world besiege us,
Ending with the dawning of the last day of the war as foreigners.

Héctor de la O – MAR 06

Remember, "infidel" is a relative term.

8.

Folklore lady like a flower child twenty years before
Rebellion taught the world to rock – But who began
In 1910 when you were three? Francisco I. Madero.
Doesn't treachery go hand-in-hand with destiny,
And don't you feel betrayed since you turned six?

Kaleidoscopic pain delivered you from childhood,
As eighteen inches of cold steel a maiden violated,
Hardening your heart as iron was annealed in blood,
Leveling your sights against a friend who never was;
Or can this mortal plane your friendship count as good?

H.d.l.O – FEB 06

You cannot judge
but what you comprehend.
So let her rest in peace –
and may God have mercy
on us all.

9.

I'll tell you how Guillaume Picard came down to Spain,
Defeating all Islam round about Segovia for a home:
Evoke and summon up your ghosts to tell a tale anon;
Nobility rekindle now the bravery that was shown,
To stoke the fires of the faith of men once more,
If not the flames of ire lay us all to waste today,
To claim our souls who but for God's own faith in us,
Young blood should cease to flow but leave a stain.

Now join the mission of a faithful few to find again
Our blessed origins, for Gentiles had it known:
Christianity was not a title but emblazoned on a crest,
Resounding from the defenders' hearts in battle cries
In days of old no less avowed in our own time.
So go to the tree www's to find your name impressed
In registries of noble men to whom we owe our lives,
Sustained by their intrepid deeds until our day was won.

H. d. l. O – 01 FEB 06 – Aleluyah! –

10.

They're all alike down to the mole and personality,
Hand-cut and tempered in the fires that abound,
Ethereally at first and then material as the clay,
Resembling one another to confuse all but the Potter,
Everyone a carbon copy like a brazen stereotype.

Every time a temptress stirs my soul to sin I see
Xena and her warrior mother's sisters of the Celts;
In a world of lovely women anyone but daughters.
Smoky Mountains, Appalachians, Cookson Hills aside,
Today beware you not fall prey to doppelgangers' whims.

Tonight show Johnny how to marry look-alikes:
Young Joanna left Joanne outside the mirror's frame;
Placebos make you feel the same as fifty mikes.
Each time a new one's made she tries to break the mould,
So watch yourself – you don't look hard to duplicate.

H.d.l.O – 31 JAN 06

It's true – "Why settle for second best", they tend to say – But what about a reasonable facsimile! You never can tell, maybe the dupe is better that the real McCoy. I'd rather have the spittin' image on my arm, "than to have never loved at all"

I tell you, the names have been changed (to protect the insolent), but every other aspect, right down to mannerisms, is the same; it's uncanny! Carbon copies named Yolanda, playful as a kitten purring so seductive, even Kimberlies, down to their olive eyes, in the middle of some magazine.

Just watch and see – Even Pepe told me I reminded him of
some buddy from Morelos, same voice and sense of humor, etc.
Whatever – Just another modern-day phenomenon. We have filled
the earth; there are so many of us now, why re-invent the wheel?!
Just crank 'em out now that we think we got one right!

11.

Fifteen centuries their ships lit up the jungle mountainsides,
Restoring faith in Heaven in a time of human pridefulness;
On the legend of the travelers only God alone can quantify,
More countless yet the galaxies where mankind could abide.

The devils came millennia before They first embodied man;
How could the Lord allow the habitation of our birthright,
Eons before be Spectator to monstrous carnage on our shores,
Miasmic though the field of play, one day to ply their plan.

Then giant spiders spanned the plains and monkeys played,
High enough atop the world so that in Heaven they could see,
Immeasurable but to those denizens not soon to utter praise,
Spirits and then visitors who held such things at aught in awe.

Somewhere in my heart of hearts I feel a world exists above,
Its coordinates as tangible as the axioms to NASA engineers,
Grace-filled and not bereft of goodness nor accursed as we are,
Navigating for a lifetime, but not theirs, to reach another sphere.

Technology is touted for the heights we have attained,
Historically our earthen lot ascending up the escalade of time;
Epochs far beyond our gains another race like ours exists,
Yielding not to serpents in the trees, thus living unrestrained.

Come now to the Master in whose knowledge kindness reigns,
Or come to realize why we really can't use all our brains;
Muck and mire of the decadent millennia hinder ever soul,
Enabling the demons full domain to hinder even our ascent.

Don't wonder at the UFO's or angels' hands to bending corn,
Or turn to gaze upon the firmament in hopes of looking past,
When long ago they told us of the signs that should appear;
Nazca being but a mere reflection of celestial enterprise.

Too fantastic are the other-worldly beings we tend to televise,
Heads so bulbous and appendages too weak to hold a spade,
And how can love be consummated trading lust for intellect?
The real ones are as perfect as the angels and as passionate.

Kaleidoscopic myriads of stars beyond the mist and morning light,
Inhabited by innocents innocuous to pain and suffering and death,
New worlds each day are born again, their people's love to test;
Did you see them yet traverse our atmosphere, they, the meek?

Héctor de la O – 14 MAR 06

12.

Put my pintails and my mallards in a row before the pool,
And put to rest the burden of all beholden fools;
Youth and poverty as well as ignorance are deadly tools.

Though age and riches hand-in-hand should go,
Heinous is this usury, the custody of souls,
Emboldening the creditor, the debtor to grow old.

Most of us upon the earth will never make the grade;
Advancing age a predator will see us to our graves,
Nevermore allowing us our fortunes to be made.

Advance unto the battleground, all Bretons to your pike,
Lest Abaddon, before your dreams come true, your life
Lay waste, availed by ignominy, your history to spite.

H. d. l. O – 27 OCT 05

13.

In a world of left and right I'll take the latter way,
Am I ever meant to spite politicos, dichotomies,
Marked by matters of our bloody flags unfurled?
Gaze into my rationale more clear than crystal balls:
Over to the right the sheep are out to pasture free,
Not so the goats whose fate is to be left aside.
Nobody would deny the knowledge of what's right
And wrong – And wrong or right who's left behind?

Whose rights are trod-upon by leftist demagogues,
Although the right has Hitler, Pinochet and Bush?
Left-handed people too maligned are a minority,
Known to normal folks for their innate anomaly,
Label something sinister and it is seen as evil,
Instead the righteous, on the other hand, are good.
Know this too, that when your frame of mind is right,
Exactly at the right place and time, we have propinquity.

Though in the northern hemisphere a left-hand spin
Heaves the hurricanes and maelstroms all around,
Even if my Chinese neighbors meet and pass me,
Clock-wise shall I take my turns about the park,
Like a metal-cutting carbide bit that cuts on through,
Only to the right, or all that's left is backing out of it,
Count in electric fans and pedaling bikes and Earth,
Kinetically awhirl each day or there would be no night.

Then you sense the axis twirl within some twilight trip,
Hoping that you're right as rain when morning comes
Earthbound a-spin atop the big blue carousel awhirl,
Put into perspective, everything is right or used to be,
Or perhaps there is but one thing left to set a-right:
Light years lost forever – the logic of our time unwound,
Eternity will happen right around the bend of time,
So near and yet so far – so right and yet so wrong.

And now the Left turns to the Right by Muscovite demand,
River Jordan does the Seine believe your right bank gauche?
East is East and West is West is all so geographical,
Right hand doing still its all to spite the left hand's intellect.
It leaves me but to ponder on the reason of this rhyme;
Get it right his Lordship said, and we can work it out;
How other than from left to right the writing of a line,
To end these musings now, I'm left to think, is only right.

H. d. l. O – Nonsense!
25 April 06

14.

Aren't we as alive asleep as when we are awake?
But I would venture all the more so as we take
Our rest from the attention of a highly-focused mind,
Until the pain behind our eyes somehow assuaged,
Then will our spirits roam untamed by space and time.

My life is fraught with ills and still I conquer evil,
Yonder past the threshold of my waking battlefield;
Obsidian is the blade of night upon whose edge,
Without inconstant inhibition to negate our escapades,
Navigating through the night's expanse we save the day

Doubting if our exploits in that world were memories,
Or somnolent episodes in nether-worldly ports-of-call,
Until our dying day of one thing we are certain:
Be the essence of the form we took ethereal or dense,
The habitation of that cosmic plane we will forever claim.

In my teenage years I wrote of hellish elevator rides,
Nihilistic in my Never-land of warring neighborhoods,
Traversing tangled zip codes interwoven in their strife,
Harboring ancient hatreds hailing us in honor's name,
Even to the gates of hell for want of better worlds.

Reality is no more tangible nor any less than dreams,
Evolving from some vaporous image into men and steel,
And the fire and thunder than can but awaken sleepers
Leaps into the atmosphere identical but deadly now,
More real than the Manhattan Melodrama's epilogue.

Over time someone will tell you that she had a dream,
Forewarning you from such or such an enterprise,
To bring the fear of Daniel to your door at once.
However free of superstition fiercely you purport to be;
Each soul is interlinked to every other like a fabric.

Did the wounds of nightmares awaken you with pain?
Recall the reason for those bruises you now bear,
Evidence that lycanthropes abound amidst the twilight,
Absent-minded actors on an empty theater's unlit stage,
Mindless episodes in life comingled with our dreams.

What is fact or fiction and what again is fantasy,
Or the reveries of madmen with delusions of grandeur?
Regard again recurring nightmares warning us of doom:
Lying in our bed or walking – what is real and what a dream,
Did you hear me talking in your sleep and learn the truth?

H. d. l. O – 16 NOV 05

15.

Bin Laden's gone and scurried like a dog in Pakistan,
Under Afghan suns and moons so confident his hand.
Saddam in his own home became a stranger to despise,
Hung up on a dollar he once had now buried in a hole.

Sons are born and some are too soon lost;
Enough are taken in the street beside a bomb.
Now terrorists arise to fill the devil's ranks,
To buckle on eternity by martyrdom so fleet.

Too soon a Texan bears his arms to fight;
He should have followed Don Corleones's lead to offer
Enmity should Sunnidom refuse to toe the line;
Meanwhile cries of "Semper Fi" resound among the graves.

And now the coffers cannot pay for our lost prestige,
Where even oil atoned for slighted diplomats abroad,
As acts of God lay siege to modern-day Gomorrahs,
You and I attest to history before our very eyes.

H. d. l. O – DEC 05

The little horn that goes into perdition (Osama, or Obama?) – or do
we have to wait 'til Dubya bites the dust? Who can fight against
the Beast? How can Babylon face up to Babylon the Great?
Another Viet Nam? Just wait until we bring the boys back home!

Just like the boys from Hanoi were waiting on the outskirts of Saigon until the final helicopter lifted off, the Sunnis and the Shias will unite but to defeat the Kurds – but, Oh, watch out for Baghdad! Classic big-stick tactics undermine their land, and only some Americans can see! U.S.M.C.

Oh, yeah, what's this "laissez faire" some think is happening from Up Above? Not so. Mr. Zimmerman said, "I'm only a pawn in their game", so "It's all in the game". It is all part of the Master Plan. Stand by for details.

16.

And when shall I be at a loss for words of truth,
Compounded to upset the local pedantry somewhat,
Rife with terse banality and blatant quasi-prose,
Of such pedestrian quality it seems like Rooney,
Sixty minutes of what my ego deems my saving grace,
Turned to saving face by circumventing time again,
Immersing memory in strife until a verse emerge,
Clip-and-paste from the date base of outer space.

Did you read Shakespeare, Joyce & Tennyson or Keats?
Of all the four I love the Bard of Avon's travesties;
Give me lovers turned to fighters for the sake of love,
Given to emotional excess each one of us when young.
Every lover's knuckles and all fighters' hearts bear wounds.
Regard all poets as presumptuous for their subtle insight;
Look me up and down and down on me but look me up.

H. d. l. O – DEC 05

17.

Actions speak louder than words – Good-bye, dear!
'Cause he's never coming home from work again,
'Cause this time he, through no fault of his own,
Is really leaving – You'll find him in his bier.
Did he take his wallet? Hope he didn't damage it!
Every day he fills his pockets heading for the door;
Numerous, yea, endless times he'll empty them again,
Though the final time they'll put it all into a plastic bag.
And of us all each day some will go spinning off,
Launched into the void beyond a deadly impact,
Limp and lifeless garments left lying just outside the door;
Yonder the dimensional horizon – beyond it no one cares.

On this side: All colored lights and howling, honking vehicles;
Near that final exit an incessant drip-drip-dripping,
Then the coffee's done at work and one cup's left,
Hanging on the pegboard with some chocolates and a note;
Eventually they'll take it down and will recall the day,
Free to celebrate again some new and meaningless event.
Right now you slumber in a dark and dreamless sleep,
Every now and then your image crossing over to us,
Entertaining the emotions and deceiving the perceptions;
Wives and other temporal companions like some animals,
Always feel like some undying yet now useless instinct.
You oblivious will sleep through their entire lifetimes,
Survivors they to the crosses and the ribbons at the roadside.

18.

How come you did what you did to him last night?
Oh you can chalk it up to mob mentality for now,
Mobsters never falter from the code of nonconformity,
Except at home at night before they sleep they pray;
But if they ask for blessings, who shall minister to them?
Only fallen angels with their unwashed faces answer
Youths more temporal than they, but as condemned
Someday to face the fire, their sinful wounds unhealed.

All the comedy now ridicule, and pleasure turned to pain,
Retribution goes beyond the suffering of drive-by death;
Each unrepentant act will crease your consciousness,
Atonement never was entire for the Hail Marys offered.
Lying draped across a picket fence is Dickiebird recalled,
On Judgement Day to point out murderers in the dock.
Neighborhood processions will parade before the Judge;
Every triggerman will walk his final steps out to the lake.

In the dark your victim's shadows meld into your prayers,
Not a soul shall interfere with your solicitous soliloquy,
Token words arise amidst the din of victims' dying agonies,
Humor-like to fog the memory of the surviving witnesses;
Expired hence but soon to wake and bring the dead to life,
Eternal only to the innocents who grace the gallery today.
Now the silence of your advocate is final; your accomplices,
Detractors now, await with you to hear your sentences.

19.

All day long we played the main stage in Seattle,
Right up until the end of Monday afternoon;
Remember that we had to be in Salem early Tuesday?
In the interim between the final show and sundown,
Various artists slamming pounders at the Expo pub,
Endured the tippling of their tankards to a man.

Soon enough we had to hit the road like troupers,
Out of town and southward bound in spite of hours
Well-spent before the mic throughout the weekend,
Every May for three-day weekends 'til the accident'
Let me reminisce with Pepe, who was snatched away,
Lying in the arms of Morpheus, by Abaddon himself.

Rend the mantle that divides the highway from a dream,
Enduring hundreds of nocturnal miles, Spartan-like, I wake
So that my cross not grace in anonymity some milepost.
Tell the host of Heaven when I nap to watch me on my way,
Enlivening my eyes each second that I lapse into the Zone,
Detouring me from dreams to tread a wakeful mile again.

H. d. l. O – 25 OCT

20.

Bone-dry desert and the peaceful silence rules the plain;
Of a sudden the monsoon drowns the countryside,
May God have mercy on the mindless skies.
But how the water floods the beaten path again,
And never strays so far it cannot bring your house to ruin
So sure the innocents who hear it fall won't drown?
The nature of the beast is to empower the image
It portrays, not so unlike an ancient river's flow
Celerity displays and ceases never to deliver all
Its water to the sea and then it rains again
Tomorrow or the next day with a torrent uncontrolled;
Yet thus our words will trickle and then flood the land.

21.

Dormant images align themselves to wakefulness,
Remnants each of episodes of somnolent sport,
Each dream the mortal shade beyond the lunar light.
Astride the midnight mare I told you once about,
More men have met their Maker in the dead of night.

Pass the Buck and place your bets – the game begins:
Lay down the life you knew today and say a prayer
Abaddon who never sleeps has no designs on your demise;
Cenotaphs can grace the dreamscape while your soul,
Egressing to the land of love and light can live another day.

Eventide and as we drift away the classic scenes replay,
Visual as reality the remnants of a darkened memory,
Every bit as vivid and as tangible as truth revisited again,
Reliving moments like an unavoidable recurring masquerade,
You and I unwitting members of a captive audience engaged.

Now must we perform in a reality without director's vision,
Immersed in a production, never conscious of its premise,
Goaded on, restrained of impotence whose edge materializes
High unto a fortnight in an unavoidable and parallel reality,
Transforming once fictitious ethers into deadly deja-vu.

APRIL 08

22.

Juarez isn't worthy, nor Nogales or Tijuana,
Up against the highly-valued cities of the South,
And the poor unfortunates born farther north,
No place among the native sons legitimacy find.

Evict them all who disavow a State so welcoming,
Lying in wait to claim the mercies of another land,
If in their own today no lack of crime or famine
And injustice plied against the nearest to malign,
Stirs a patriot to leap the crenels enveloped in a flag.

H. d. l. O – 10 JUN 08

23.

Poor dying ember in the sway of your abomination,
Ordered like a punk to light the finite world so gaily!
Languishing in limbo while the wheels of justice turn,
And the sands of time drift down through the abyss,
Never ends tomorrow where forever's phase begins.
Curve your will before the truth is overcome by lies;
Only you can find your way through liberty's excess.

JUN '08

24.

Pity flaming embers used to light abomination's pyre,
Oblivious to their finite glow like fruitage falsified,
Living out their usefulness and cast aside like punks,
As the sands of time drift down through the abyss,
Never's name remaining 'til tomorrow's day begins.
Curve your will before the truth is overcome by lies;
Only we can liberate our lives from liberty's excesses.

H. d. l. O – 10 JUN 08

25.

A generation before Cholos weren't we "Spanish"?
No one after Fremont's folly deigned to call us "Mexican".
Don't you recollect they pulled them off the streetcars,
When they caught them draped like Southland Calloways?
Herded like the hostage infidels of old Hispania relived,
Amounting to mere boys too proud to melt in the milieu,
Trumping dress codes and decrees of solidarity with thieves.
It was so with your Miss Clay from El Sereno School,
Sniffing at our hair pomade like an angry Lois Lane.
My Spirit grieved at hatred with a beautiful face;
You wonder at such symbiosis with enduring xenophobes.

Never did I heed the haughty admonitions of John Wayne,
And so the hyphen joins my pride to my identity with you,
Though Totonacs cold never share equality with Aztecs.
If the nannies put on airs, the gardeners will take up arms!
Once again the mother tongue of immigrants is pre-Columbian.
Nobody but they can understand what Oscar de la Hoya feels,
And your divisive nature like the Aztec arrogance of old,
Laid bare like mortal wounds that signaled their demise,
In the twinkling of an eye can thus expose your token state.
Then I wonder, as the Hand of God dries up the Rio Grande,
Yonder does an iron fence divide the truth from Destiny.

H. d. l. O – 24 JUN 08

26.

Someone has to teach the lowly-birthed
Of the meaning of true love and kindness,
Cancelled by all earthly evil that is laden
On the backs of the endemic retinue,
Regarded by the best as lesser-thans,
Reviled as fair game by the antithesis
Of everything esteemed and also vilified.

Redeemed as I have felt from the beginning,
Awarded if unmeritoriously by Providence,
Memory not fail me lest I be the more remiss,
If once to visit you when you were ill I lacked,
Relegating you to suffer thence abandoned death.
Evil sin besides I could not ever claim for worse;
Zero from the first should be my recompense.

All hail the truth!

H. d. l. O – 23 SEP

27.

Beauty like the women of the fjords,
Lovely as the Finnish in the North,
Amidst the women of the Arizona sun,
Inimitable you are and unapproachable;
Rely on this your gift to travel far afield.

Of your soul partake to share its grace;
None but the good can ever hope achieve
Eternal recognition for the life we live.
I on the threshold of old age do yet extol,
Lacking not for sight as I behold, your image.

H. d. l. O – JUN ’08

28.

His father told of Pancho Villa's days,
Emancipated from the hold of fear of death.
Commanded by the protocol of strength;
Tormented by temptations length and breadth
Ordained to test the limits of his faith,
Regard this new Picard as faithful yet.

H. d. l. O – JUN 08

Semper fidelis Deus est.

29.

Darlings of the sparkling atmosphere who've paid
Entrance fees to the demise of consciousness,
Cancel now your membership to the forsaken.
At only minutes from the closing of the compass,
Draw the circle shut and take your place outside;
Enclosed remain the members of a caste derided
Nearly six millennia, so fill and raise the final cup,
Their blood like aged wine to spill for your delight.

Now gaze upon the epilogue like prayers to recall,
Entreating the return to reason at the equinox.
While hope as dreams shall in the nighttime stay,
With the dawn of the eternal day to then arise,
Of all anticipation freed at last, no call again to fear
Regression to a life of vital faith and futile perfidy,
Lay down your weapons in a war you never won;
Delight yourselves in nothing until everything is done.

H. d. l. O – JAN '08

30.

Johnny was a madman from the El Sereno hills,
On matters of philosophy expounding to the world
His M.O. like a modern Socrates to spite himself;
Notions like a crystal walkway to the moon are signs,
When he smacked his grandma down for smirking,
And his mother and her Chinaman committed him,
Don't you remember how we felt compassion flame,
Each time they hooked him up for shocking therapy?

Loco was his nickname and we answered to the same,
On a scale from one-to-ten, we were thirteen homeboys
Never far from mustard-covered hills and acid trips,
Gulping gallons of Italian table wine from Big Joe's store.
Given to the neighborhood prescription, we medicated
On the hillside overlooking Huntington, unsupervised,
Never far from the adventure of the parties or the river,
Every one of us so firmly planted in our permanence.

For a time we broke him out of Garfield Avenue on visits,
Rocking khakis and Sir Guys, all uniform including Johnny,
Often all of us identical we marched him out the door,
Mistaken for each other like a cavalcade of crazies all-for-one.
His father fought with Rommel when he and Johnny's mom,
On his furloughs found each other in Berlin until she fled;
Mexicans were sent to concentration camps with gypsies.
Every human has his origins and every history its life.

So I went away to war and Johnny went to prison for assault;
On an outing with my buddies in Tijuana, Johnny sat behind
Me like a secret shadow from my past, a sojourner like us all,
Eons from the days we shared beyond the exit of the 710.

Today he lies beneath the ground another victim of the times;
It was easy to reject our very lives as undesirable back then,
Many of my equals found the gate to their eternal rest
Eventually, like a novel leaving readers doubtful of a sequel.

H. d. l. O – MAY '09

31.

Too close and shall I taste your dulcet breath.
Oh, come and let me hold your slender waist;
Recalling how you grace that jersey dress.

32.

Delay me not to know how you have fared,
All these years since you were seventeen;
I pray all thirty-three have brought you love;
Derelict I'd be but for this springtime wish:
And that is that these fifty bring you joy,

H. d. l. O – 22 FEB 08

33.

Sunshine burning on the faces of the brave,
To warm their hearts enjoining them to fight.
Rouse yourselves – the battle's at the door!
Inspired to want for nothing, like all men,
Kindred of the lowly members of our station,
Each one of us as insular as grains of sand,
Residents of one same life as in the sky the stars,
Shining every one his light forth all as one.

And Eva, Vicki and their sister Silvia danced
Raptly with a passion to the rhythm of the drums,
Echoing across the courtyards this frenetic din.
But to the men in power money merits sweat;
Rubber-stamping minions at the Judge's table sit,
And fill their bellies while we pound the cobblestones,
Very soon the Jubilee will take the place of holidays,
Every man employed to build another's home no more.

H. d. l. O – 22 OCT 07

34.

As I tumbled down the southern Magic Mountainside,
Borne aloft, the churning smoke encountered me,
A cloud of hydrocarbon death amid the atmosphere,
Yonder hailing to the Mt. St. Helens gases roiling
Onward through the surface streets so Herculanean,
Fetid, acrid, choking poison packing pulmonary cavities.

Similes, hyperboles and metaphors allowing me,
Maybe I'm exaggerating nightmarish scenarios,
O.K.! But who can clearly see from 1st to 7th Street?
Knowledge of the smog alerts anticipate the toll.
Every morning that the Pompeii populace awoke,
Subtracted one more day of life, and so it is for us.

If I do not smoke, why does it hurt to breathe?
Sucking wind begrudgingly in tiny, burning gulps?
Today, we live with vestiges of what Vesuvius was,
Hanging like a Damoclesian blade, impending, ominous:
It's the inversion layer Jillian always gurgles over,
Slowly smoking us like herring in a basin by the sea.

Héctor de la O – 08 JUL 02

35.

In the end they say all things will be confused,
So shouldn't there be room for contradiction still?
Right atop our logic, the laws of nature always one.
Ascending far beyond the rules of gravity my goal,
Escaping from the masses mired in the status quo,
Lacking never for the love of truth let us transcend:

Are words as these not easy to vouchsafe for idleness?
Regarded to be disregarded by the riders of the new wave,
Every "truth", nonetheless must have some equal parallel,
To whet the appetite of bodhisattvahs starving in the void.
However tethered we may seem to be to the modernity,
Ephemeral those bonds that tie us to the trend; Awaken!

Clouds of smoke and mirrors and red herring to deter,
Hinder nothing but that moment that you were delayed;
Or keep endorsing the reports that grace our every dawn,
Satisfied the spin the messenger has given them is gospel.
Enter now the plastic panic-stricken public's rash opinions;
Now the very armies of the living God must seek atonement.

Put in terms so plan the eyes of the potatoes can discern,
Either Jaweh Jireh or Allah will set the stage to dry the rivers,
Or you haven't seen the forest where there used to be no trees?
Portentously the oceans rise and winter bends to summer's will;
Languishing like water-lapping hydrophobes we only hear these
Ever-present rumors of the end to be where the beginning was.

36.

Ride toward the beach along the south side of the iron fence,
Obliged to make a left three hundred meters from the sand,
So near and yet so far from the corners of the coastal shore,
And head southward on the curving asphalt strand,
Ride on, between the hillsides and the intermittent domes,
Imitating the resplendent whiteness of the Andalusian South,
To wend alongside bony settlements disjointed by the cliffs,
Overgrown with succulents and fennel in the ocean breeze.

Before the turnoff to the scenic road an old arroyo flows,
Ever standing past the bridge the horses tethered still,
And the skinny cowboy wearing sandals grins at us,
Chewing chili mango on a chopstick with his golden teeth.
Heaven is eternal blue and islands shelter foreign ships,
Motionless and tiny on the leeward side of the volcanic rocks.
Every block the pharmacies, the seafood bars and artisans abound,
XLNT the Mexican colonial style of
common wood with varnish glints.

What about the concrete fountains and the decorated benches,
Encrusted with mosaics of shards of crockery the Indian lady made?
Little known to many is the town's renown for the indigenous dishes:
Corn tamales, sweet and gold, and tacos and tostadas full of fish.
On the dusty roadside copper kettles shine, and iron smelling,
Metal-sounding shops keep on hammering out the gates and railings
Every smithy a museum, some repositories of the rusted, unsold
Sculptures abandoned like so many orphans left unclaimed.

H. d. l. O. - 2008

37.

Did you set the thermostat to spite the bloody Raj,
Environmentally, like to the polar opposite of Limbo?
Patrons of the "JAC" eschew the fires of Gomorrah,
As they raised the flesh to blisters like a chicharrón.
Relative as all things are again, the beauty of the snow
Tends to lose its luster to a sleepy, snowbound dog.
Meant to grace a landscape like a vision from afar,
Enveloped in the ice or fire neither would an option be,
Nor does my sense of duty warm to such a nice place,
Tethered to the Dog Town foundry while the cases run.

Everybody feels the cold with which we daily do contend;
If walls are welcome boundaries to the inclement miasma,
Get your bearings as to where the frozen realm extends,
Harsh as hoarfrost on the whiskers of the wayward in Alaska,
Temperate on the other hand, outside the walls of C-JAC.
Young and old I see a band of brothers chilling in hoc loco;
Dash outside; the gallery en masse is making a mad dash
To get relief not only from the man the law commissions,
Whose icy judgements from the mindless cogs churn out,
Obstinate as stone and cold as what an ice house renders.

H. d. l. O – 07 JUL 09

(Commissioner John W. Green has a cough)

38.

Jocund as the gelato girl until she's out of limes,
Egregious as the roaring lion at the end of time.
Secure as the queen mother sitting on her beast,
Surrounded by her retinue of thieves of jubilees.
Inviolate her sense of might though right abandon her;
Can cliffs albeit of stone defy the salton aquifer,
And despots by contumely survive the march of time?

Images of lovers rising from the flames of vengeance,
Savoring disincarnate visages of fleshly recompense.
Cancelling these mental escapades a laborer awakens,
Renouncing reveries, his sense of wrong unshaken.
Unbeknownst to renegades who perpetuate injustice,
Everybody else can see to what their end's entrusted,
Like enemies of musketeers and Locksley's evil nemesis.

H. d. l. O – 26 AUG 08

39.

Dust from the Northland on the soles of your feet,
Each one of you so lucky that you didn't have to meet
A member in good standing of the Neighborhood Elite,
Tenacious of his living space and safety his streets;
He'd never hand over the key to highwaymen or thieves.

So now your own authorities are washing their hands;
Quick! Hide yourselves or fall prey to the justice of the land,
Unless you fear no danger from that age-old evil band.
And still you shave your head and let your trousers sag;
Develop some respect for law and jump out of the gang.

H. d. l. O - @2007

40.

All of us were chosen once to walk the earth;
Believing in the reason for our being is the why,
Or is it essential to be conscious of our living?
Really, don't we suffer every day that we exist?
Tenacious though our grip, our grasp is tenuous,
Immediacy not being as clear as history is real.
Our future on the other hand is purely probable;
No less it is our lot in life to live in spite of fear.

If we never saw the light of day were we so less alive,
So that our spirit like a specter could not be revived?
And so they do not thrive who cannot claim a birth,
Whether there be dearth of all the attributes of man.
Regard the woman who is conscious of another life
Other than her own within herself throughout her time,
Never faltering for lack of faith she'll see her progeny,
Given the premeditated peril to a being yet to be.

Héctor de la O – 08 JUL 04

"Isn't it strange that all the people in favor of abortion,
Have been born already?"

41.

They travel in the company of beauties ever more,
Humiliating all unwary interlopers in their deeds,
Emasculating some while others they eviscerate,
Until these crash unconsummated in their enterprise.
Gratified but hardly ever if the matron has her way.
Laboring on they falter in the sowing of their seed,
Yet do these suitors never to be known still tarry

But to chaperone the lovelies is their mission in this life:
If not for them, intact whose honor would remain?
Too many of their cohorts' passions could ignite,
Carrying in an erstwhile empty heart a torch in it.
Harboring memories now of passing handsome boys,
Every brazen call of hail-thee-maiden nothing gained,
Someday you'll learn to walk alone if I am fortunate.

Héctor de la O – 7 JUL 04

"Why do they always look at you;
How come they never look at me?"

42.

And you think you're funny clowning me?
Regal as an Uma with a Vegas poker face,
Immobile as a Roman spectator to witness
Ghastly mayhem but you'll never raise a pinkie
In defense of anyone beyond appointed clients,
Darling meretrix devoid of tender mercies.

Frosty as the night beyond the reach of pilots,
Reminiscent of a type-cast Nazi prison nurse,
Incandescent eyes and lips as cold as steel:
Gypsum has more color that the pallor seen
Irradiating from the thinness of your skin,
Defender of the criminals, Oh, sister Mary B.!

Bridle my berating tongue and straighten my bent;
Resolve to show the truth unnoticed heretofore:
Imbedded in the sallow clay so hard to cultivate,
Gentility perchance abides as in an unknown land?
Intransigent to form a friendship foreign heretofore,
Doubtless may your swinging gait still welcome me?

H. d. l. O – 02 AUG 06

43.

Soft and rounded as a painted Chinese cloud,
Her pink lips were like the petals of a rose,
And delicate as Ziyi Zhang with almond eyes,
Regarding me with Zen-like innocence;
Oh, why in my naiveté should I today fall prey?
Now languishing in reveries of but a tender kiss.

I shall repent of beauty not to be possessed;
New dreams shall fill the night until the day
Our name is blessed for love we truly knew.
Unassuming with your gentle gaze and smile,
Young as you and I were oh so long ago,
Each of us no less believed in life's eternity.

H. d. l. O – 28 AUG 06

44.

Tie-ups on the thoroughfares should be avoided;
Hometown avenues the natives know to go around.
Every now and then I'll find myself again,
Around the corner from a major traffic jam,
Lined up north and south and east and west four-deep,
Pointing toward the middle like a swarm of hungry fish,
In a feeding frenzy victimizing those pedestrians
Newly joined to us from places lacking intersections,
Empty-headed transients wading into evil streams
So nonchalant you'd think they were forewarned:
The right-of-way is ironclad as an imperial decree!

Cathay Motors sold another rice machine today;
Liability is of no concern where money is no object.
Uniformity to be attained or bear the Yangtze stigma,
Senior citizens' senility and frightened girls' rigidity
Take a back seat to the driver with a Reagan pompadour,
Eclipsed in turn by sausage-fingered red-light bandits,
Rolling through the city in a county-furloughed caravan.
Finding parking at high noon on New High St. at Ord?
Unless you take North Spring and double back to College,
Can you differ from the sailor who can never reach a port,
Kung Pao chicken wafting through the smoky cluster-fuck.

H. d. l. O – 05 JUN 07

45.

Gary, I don't dream about you anymore;
Eventually, you lost the fight your rival won.
Rebellion from the laws of nature quelled,
Another one bites the dust intoned the queen,
Rhapsodizing the demise of wanton cannibals
Destiny has claimed for self-inflicted crimes,
Orphans desolate and mothers crying, home alone.

Marines in battle never knew such bravery;
Of your exploits only your companions can recall,
None of which remain but in the cells or tombs,
Thus ending the careers of others of your ilk.
Even old Mrs. McComb could see the consequences
Retribution would inflict one day for disobedience,
On reprobates who've never learned to value life.

H. d. l. O – 28 AUG 06

46.

My son lives on an acre in the City of Peace
On a fertile tract of land over an ancient stream.
Wet and wild underground it rushes toward the West,
Somewhere near where the Willamette turns away.

Today I saw him shining like the northern sun,
Henry Weinhard in one hand and the other on the wheel,
Advancing on the parkland green with a resolve
That only youth whose future lies ahead could feel.

Liberty and Fortune, Oh, take me to my children's home,
Away from Southland shores and stranger solitude,
Where we can thus await the coming of the final days,
Nearer hearth and kin and far from Destiny's detours

Who has ever seen me with my pocket empty, when,
Instead the Universal Providence conveyed me upward,
To the light of Wisdom from the folly of Ignominy,
Hammered at the forge of Life and honed by Time.

Someone take me to the Treasury today to meet my son,
Or test my funds and I shall kick some down to you,
Money that we seldom lack and everybody's healthy;
Effervescent joy to spare and riches ever measuring.

Baking in the valley sun the golden barley knows,
Each blade of common pasture grass would that it were
Equal to it as the Marion berry vines and strings of hops
Rise up in the Abbey's rows to flavor Thompson's brew.

H. d. l. O. – 01 JUN 07

47.

Gospel number one, chapter second-to-the-last,
Hinders not a general belief that spirits walk
On earth, as well as we of more substantial form.
Subscribe to what you will as I to Matthew's verse;
Tomorrow's television fiction shall be documented fact,
So much more so than the premonitions of Jules Verne.

If the prophets' prayers that the sun delay its course
Held fast the light of day, the slaughter to prolong,
And another one gave witness to a prophesy fulfilled,
Very soon the world will see another resurrection, "live";
Eyewitness News shall disavow the paparazzi's claims,
As two men who spoke against the world and died arise.

Though you deem these words untrue, I spoke them not;
However, I avow with heartfelt credit the reliable accounts
Eyewitnesses relayed of those whom they had known who died,
Of maidens, saints and Lazarus who walked again among us,
Regardless of the rot their bones had suffered by demise;
You judge if whom you see is angel, demon, ghost or man.

H. d. l. O – 06.13.07 – (Exhibit A)

48.

Never answer when I ask you where you've been.
"Anywhere but where the likes you can find me";
Did you perceive in me a whit more than concern?
I'll not play Roger Rabbit to your Jessica once more,
Nor beg you pretty-please to notice that I'm burning,
Every time I play the fool to turn my eyes toward you.

You mix where you have been with where you are,
Or trade the freed men for the ones you've set at large,
Unless you think your ditzy moves your saving grace.
Around the corner from your weekends on the bay,
Resides the destiny reserved for certain single mothers,
Evicted from their independent lifestyle, unemployed.

Presumptuous and so I pay the price for prideful lust,
Regretting never having been indulged by idol-prey.
Each time I've lost in love I count the cost as just
The price a fool must pay for soaring toward the sun.
The object of my predilection come to set me straight,
You charge admission to an outrage as it were for fun.

Pack your baggage and book passage on your own,
Oppress another border pirate with your booty's heft,
Imagine that it's raining men up to your hip bones,
So that it looks as though another victim more or less,
Or either passengers or stowaways won't tip your boat –
Now get over your fine self and let me love again, ha-ha!

02 JUN 07

49.

Forty-nine millennia they sailed the monstrous main,
Actively pursuing a carnivorous melee aground as well.
Later, they appealed to the ambition of our matriarch,
Lying through his teeth, the father of them all, to her,
Endeavoring to put an end to promises of paradise,
Nullifying blessings with a simple bite to prove intent.

And in those days there was no rain upon the earth,
Nor deserts, but a lush expanse of humid green;
Gone to seed, our generation shone for loveliness,
Each one of them with no resistance took our girls,
Like chattel giving to their masters as a profit,
Sons and warriors of renown until the holy flood.

H. d. l. O – 21 JUN 07

If you die first,
We're splitting up your gear.

50.

Of all the lousy P.D.'s; why'd they have to give me you?
How the hell did you all pass the finals down at U.S.C.?
At least you could have argued down the offer some,
To convert my 60 days, to working on the freeway crew.
Tell the judge I promise to take some time off now;
It's only that I didn't want my boss to get pissed off,
Though now he's given me some leeway for a change.
Until last week, he hadn't given me a weekend free;
Don't think it's easy giving up a Sunday hangover
Eleven months to don a yellow vest at 4:00 a.m.!

Defendant so-and-so, you've brought your kids again,
Even though I told you not to bring them to the court!
Find the number to the foster home and snatch 'em up;
Extenuating circumstance is not of your creation.
Nor is it your domain to determine mercy's measure.
Did you think all judges cry on cue like television
Actors vying for the part of the protector of your spawn?
Not on your life, and I have children of my own at home.
To think I can be swayed by mindless machinations,
Senseless suppositions of compassionate relief!

Corroborate the rumors of commissioners incumbent,
Added to the rolls of re-elected scandal fodder:
New Yoricans won't de-mystify the deaths of wayward sons;
Chief reasons the authorities should have justified again
Excess torque to realign contemptuous constituents,
Leading citizens devoid of criminal intent to riot,

Somewhere in a park where no one dares to gamble
On the domino's effect on upright demonstrators.
Move the pawns, the enabling public figures, as befitting
Errant relegates of righteous indignation to their end!

H. d. l. O – 21 JUN 07

51.

I've never had to feel so violated in my life;
Put me under house arrest – see if I care,
And let me keep my live-in maid and gardener.
Remember, I'm above your travesties so vile,
I'm so sure! I feel such righteous indignation;
Stick me with a forty-five-day sentence, Judge!

How would you like living next to thirty dirty girls
In these ugly polyester jumpsuits for three days,
Like I disobeyed a Federal injunction when I took
The car just down the street to see some friends!
Or do you feel that I should turn all anti-social too?
No way! Your boys were lying in wait to frame me!

But my lawyer bought my freedom late last night,
And now Lee Baca's on the carpet one more time.
I got another summons to the court on Washington,
Like near the Staple Center, I'm so sure, and U.S.C.,
Of all the gross indignities! I've had to wash my sox
Under the watchful eye of female deputies, I'm sure,
Totally! Pay these people, Daddy – Take me home!

H. d. l. O – JUN '07

52.

Look at what the cat dragged in:
Is what you are worth who you are?
Victory for self-made men is being
Even here to claim we've gone so far!

Young men never sense the end of time;
Obituaries tend to occupy the final page,
Unless your exploits so illustriously
Reserve your story for the headline news.

Let the children shine their little light;
It is our only hope in daylight so diffuse,
For even fear of night has taken many souls,
Eclipsing our existence like a willful moon.

Rest assured you have a purpose here,
Elected as you were from the milieu.
Admitted to the mortal main we all ascend,
Like the words of history arisen from a page

H. d. l. O – 15 MAY 07

53.

When I was young I went to Viet Nam, I think,
And all the people were my friends at twenty-one.
Regardless of the dollars and piasters we exchanged,
Friendly fire from the Hill was funding Michelin
On Wall Street while we covered the plantation,
Rifling the register while the ricochets rebounded,
Over and among us, our blood comingling with the latex.
I worked the Ryukyu wharf as our ships were coming in,
Laden with our "empty-handed armies". Zimmerman.

Can we claim it all was worth the multi-flavored teas,
And the four-plies and Sriracha we enjoy today?
Not to mention long-grain, brown, and sticky rice,
Now on store shelves from Seattle to San Diego,
Or the influx of the living cargo from the sampans,
Threading down the jungle lanes toward tomorrow's land,
Whose destinies they now will share with foreigners,
In other words, with us, so bad so sad behind blue eyes.
Now the fight is for the right to burn the desert oil.

On the other hand, who says the Joneses should ascend,
Holding over us the Kalashnikov and the Kor'an?
Business being what it is, I am no slouch, Abdullah;
All I ask is that you wisely read the Revelation's verse,
Before we blunder into Babylon the Great, not ancient one;
Young lions disregard the danger of the threat and pounce.
Lying in wait outside, four horsemen hold their bridles,

Owing nothing but to put in play the Final Plagues,
Never to turn a page aback until the blessing and the curse.

Héctor de la O – 08 OCT 02

BROUGHT TO YOU BY:
THE BLAH-BLAH-BLAH NETWORK

54.

What makes you better than the rest of us?
You thought you were transparent as an extra.
Nimbly going from mark to mark you thought,
Or did you think your audience was blind,
Not noticing the sight gags you had written in,
As though your script had been approved!

You forgot about the fat guys in the balcony,
Ordering the cameras to keep on rolling,
Undeterred by the performance of your bag lady,
Gamboling through the aisles like on Supermarket Sweep,
Over-confident the part was made for you alone;
Though you played it to the hilt they didn't buy it.

But you didn't comb your hair for the judicial scene,
Unless you think you're Natalie Imbruglia today,
So full of duende notwithstanding the reviews!
This farce will falter at the box office, my dear.
Even though the courthouse segment fairly bombed,
Do you think you can still make rehearsal at Bauchet?

Hector de la O – 07 NOV 02

55.

Say it darling, what you meant to say,
Every lover to his loving sweetheart says;
Confide in me never to regret my choice,
Relate for me the details of your escapades.
Even if your words expose you, I'll display
Tolerance of faults one day to be disdained.

To know you is to know how you love me;
How ever can I ever know you perfectly?
In your thoughts you wander unaccompanied.
None but the imprudent lovers squander territory,
Gaining for their honesty but ever-failing trust,
So soon to be uncovered they, our hidden lusts.

None can be so pure of heart we couldn't shatter
Others' images of us, as thought we really mattered.
Be that as it may, as love is blind so too is rage,
Otherwise misgivings and their progeny could wage
Doubtful warfare on the battlefield of surety;
Yet so we hail integrity to hide our lack of purity.

Cover up your imperfections with a tempered tongue,
And your lack of faith subdue while you are young.
Necessity dictates the survival of a worldly few,
So bite your tongue and mind your p's and q's,
And thereby keep your love until you both are old;
You could be left without a love for being so bold.

Héctor de la O - 26 MAR 02
(True Confessions? No.)

56.

This I thought could only happen in Brazil,
Hell beginning to consume us where we live.
Each luxuriant mahogany or dusty little juniper
Yields life to an endangered race of creatures.
Carving out our own existence and our own demise,
Unlike the denizens of deserts they've reclaimed;
They guide the fountains of the deep to an oasis.

Meanwhile in the South the air is getting thin.
Younger dwellers can't remember never dressing;
They don't realize the forest clothed their fathers.
Rainfall now will wash the naked hillsides down,
Engorging riverbeds with silt to stem the flow;
Eventually the Mato Grosso's rivers will run dry,
So that entire land can know the fury of the sun

All the spectrum of the solar light comes down,
Leaking through the holes in Heaven's mantle,
Legacy of industry's elixirs going up in flames.
Densely too, a pall of smoke pervades the air
Our tiny children take into their very breast.
Whenever now you see the youthful sitting in a tree,
Noise abroad their protest of our planet's demise.

Héctor de la O – 23 MAY 02

57.

Tinsel Town has got his number and his name,
Handprints and a signature in concrete, and a star
Encrusted in the Walk of Fame down on the Boulevard.
Devoid of base sagacity beyond the mercantile bent,
Ubiquitous the clientele eyes postcards on a rack,
Kindred spirits to their counterparts in Anaheim,
Evolving from the orange orchards past the 605.

Of all our visitors a hopeful few would deign to stay,
Frozen in their tracks imagining their name in lights.

Please sirs, won't you tell me why they always come,
Abandoning the Corn belt and the wheat fields,
Determined to become the Flavor-of-the-Month?
Unlike the working class, where is their job security?
Can an unemployment check provide for therapy,
And will plastic surgery forestall a fall from grace?
High above the city someone's falling from the sign.

H. de la O – 19 JUL 02

58.

Ages ago when he was twelve years old,
Little Beto came to Bairdstown in the 60's.
But being from Durango he was tough as nails,
Even badder than his brother Joe who died,
Reveling with my brothers and the homeboys,
Tangled in the vegetation out on Big Bear Lake.

Many moons ago, you might recall the time,
On my return from Viet Nam, at Beatriz' or Irene's:
Nighttime would find us all united, partying,
Righteously as though tomorrow'd never come.
Of course it has arrived and all of us are older;
Youth has wings that fly us to our final age.

Eventually we go on SSI or Disability or die;
Life and strength abandon us to medication,
Bought on Oakland or Van Horne for pennies
Every chunk of change goes from hand to mouth,
The brass ring getting ever more elusive every turn;
Of all the riches we once had we cannot give account.

So anyway, last night he made it to my mom's;
Ever step to climb that hill on rotting feet
Reveals the character of childhood friends,
Evolving as we are into the ancients of the 'hood
Now has come the time for all good men to quit
Offending nature, luck and Providence and live!

Hector de la O – 18 JUL 02

59.

How do I close my eyes again before the dawn,
Or capture dreams that long since drifted off,
Lethargic but unwilling to succumb to Morpheus,
Entreating me to join the rest he captains well,
So that my spirit strains to flee the wakefulness.
Instead I linger in this port-of-call devoid of light,
Negated and denied a berth until the distant day.

Mount the mare of midnight madness with electric eyes,
Yearning to descend upon the day with harried riders,
Simple youths who load their sleepless years and fly,
Like Moors at the report of guns hell-bent for leather,
Every evening egging one another on with an anxiety
Equaled only by the drovers on the crystal highway,
Peppering their parting way with incandescent sand.

H. d. l. O – 09 MAY 07

60.

Then we looked before we leapt, and you too blind to see,
A thirty-two strapped on and who could get the best of me
Today this thug got a vasectomy when he reached down
The front to grip his nine and trimmed his family tree.
Others rank, and file their clique and moniker Downtown,
Or paint their pride all up and down the gothic urban scene
Epidermically, like living lampshades in the buff, and wiggle fingers
Deaf-and-dumb-like out the windows of their rice machines.

Did you know more doctors recommend not getting body-bagged?
Each time you button just the top and rock that cuff and sag,
All God's creation with a g-tag and premeditation targets all
Dead ringers for their very own except the face ain't right.
But anyways, the race to fight is aiming rockets at your peops.
Of course your due-date keeps until your shelf life ends,
Your literary contributions notwithstanding, and you're sent
Someplace where goodness, truth and light will never shine again.

H. d. l. O – 27 APR 07

61.

How come you keep shedding the blood of unknowns in the dark?
On the following morning the chalk on the pavement stays down.
Making the innocent pay, who decides which are friends or victims?
Every time that your mom sends you down to the corner for milk,
Bring your backup and strap on your nine at the door just in case
Other youths of your ilk sense your animus after you've parked;
You can shop 'til you drop – leave a lasting impression downtown,
Should your name and your face get replaced by a white silhouette.

And those things that you did will come pay you a visit one day,
Rest assured retribution is worse that reprisal – Believe it or not,
Every act unavenged can still shadow your steps to your grave,
All the way to your life's unavoidable end
just beyond youth and age.
Look at poor Dickiebird's broken remains
draped over a fence in L.A.,
Or wonder if one of his killers is somebody's grandfather now.
Never doubt one fine day they will pay for that deed every one;
Even you having died in your dotage are turning a page in a book.

In your room when you pray, as I did, are your kidding yourself?
Nothing lightens our load like confessing that we have done wrong;
Take your time to decide – Not too much – Take your place in the line.
Heaven or hell-bound, now take up your cross or keep on like before;
Every dog has his day, every sinner his wages are paid by-and-by,
Nearer too does your destiny's dawn bring your dues to the door,
Deed by deed though unseen 'til they finally send you along.

62.

Leary and his partner Owsley got it to us,
Youngest generation of the Koras and Huicholes,
Servile then to Mescalito – now to the movidas,
Entertaining novel notions rising with the tide,
Rejecting now the Spartan rancor and discord
Germane to the survival of archaic cultures:
Instead of war and hatred, love and peace abode,
Close as night and day or life and death exist,
And it tempered our existence as the hikuri did
Centuries ago when the shaman's word was law.
It was as synthetic as our respite from reality,
Dulling our senses to death and riots and the war.

Did you make that purple water for the scientist?
If so, can you imagine what it did to/for us?
Every night the sky was geometric patterns
That the great white owl traversed with engines
Humming while we laughed and drank wine on the hill,
Yearning for that nocturnal interlude so tranquilly
Lingering to lapse into tomorrow's hideous brilliance,
And assuage the vengeance of our destinies a while
Moreover that the Universal Majesties could intercede
In our behalf and earthly justice could be stayed
During the interim of our self-induced euphoria,
Effervescing from our minds like drowning victims' bubbles.

In the meantime people disappeared and left
Scintillating auras and the timbre of their voice,
And innocent sincerity shone in all our youthful eyes.
Put into perspective nonetheless it didn't matter,
If so heinous a cultural disparity did reign,

Placing in most dire jeopardy faith, hope and charity.
Episodic interdictions and selective prosecution reigned;
Despite the rhetoric of peace and love our only choice
Remained to keep our pistols at-the-ready, rocking steady
Every Greenpeace weekend by the carousel at Griffith Park,
As the heat surrounding us sweltered like hot lard,
Meaning to mix us in the stir like sunflower dumplings.

That said, what was going on besides, inside our heads?
How about angels playing harps and singing in their chariots,
As though escorting us on either flank along the freeway?
Then the faucet filled the sink with cockroaches,
Impossible to drink and only wine could keep us sober;
So too, the voices of our friends contained our sanity.
Did you ever hyperventilate and feel that you were dying?
Everybody said it was the strychnine in our liver –
And you could see a windowpane in someone's eye,
Diluted by his tears while his brainwaves melted his reality.
Later on they medicated Tommy Aguilar for dancing on the Drive;
Youth and God were dead and we failed the acid test.

Héctor de la O
"Movidas" – barrio protocol

63.

Haven't you heard of the great men of yore,
Of Romans in togas and tunics on Greeks?
Maybe they might look like sissies today,
Etruscans and Persians and Medes?
Bare-legged men wearing sandals they were,
Often called on to fight for their lives to a man.
Youth of the barrio are much more complexed:
Sandals and bare-legged shorts are not worn.

Instead their own cutoffs adhere to the norm,
No more than a foot off the sidewalk or street:
Show skin where you should have seen socks
Has you labeled for code violation, a "LOP".
On the hottest of days to wear khakis and shoes,
Really boys! Scrub the knees! Wash your feet!
The jainas however should wear Daisy Dukes,
Shorn to the pockets, with tank tops and heels

H. d. l. O – MAR 02

"LOP" – Loss of Privileges; "jainas" – "chicks"

64.

Diddyboppin' through the fifties El Sereno streets,
Images of the older boys seemed mystical to me.
Can you believe I saw his name upon a wall?
Kindred spirits were we for we too were called
In the age-old neighborhood esprit de corps,
Even at the age of twelve to do what's right
Beside our boys and stand up for the principles,
I guess, that keep all home boys indivisible:
Righteous indignation at the world beyond our own,
Dirt roads, creeks and hills in mustard flowers.

Did you know Richard fifty years ago, back then,
In that down-time before Frisko Jeens and Pendletons?
Every schoolboy knew the story of the picket fence:
Do you think it's true it was the White Fence gang.
And that they whacked and draped him over it?
No one seems to recollect those things back then –
Dickiebird – was a Pachuco like the rest of them,
Wasted in the flower of his youth by murderers,
Attracted to the smell of sacrifice like Aztec priests,
Selected to dispatch him like an executed captive.

Little do they know of fear instilled by angels:
Every crime scene has a secret Vigilant enabled,
From the Heavenly rebellion to the murdered Witnesses,
To record and list the images of every fateful deed.
Ordained to purge the punished from among us,
Now when our defenses are diaphanous at best,

Threadbare body armor sparse protection lends.
Heaven's guardians await likc stoic bailiffs,
Attentive to the order to dispense swift justice
To the killers of the innocent like Dickiebird.

Witness how they prowl the foreign avenues,
Hordes of morbid youths in dark conveyances,
Intent on the denial of mercy to all strangers,
Though their conscience scream against it.
El Sereno has its share of loved ones mourning
For sons though taken, yet whose families relive
Each moment they adorned our own existence.
Never now to be forgotten for his legend and his fame,
Certainly I shall remember Dickiebird like friends,
Even though I only knew him for his dying and his name.

H. d. l. O – 03.29.02

65.

During our nocturnal downtime there is an interlude
Reserved for mystical encounters and cosmic revelations;
Every time you doubt your very wakefulness you sleep,
And are awake when fleeting images appear as dreams;
More into the episodic deep these two conditions fuse.

Silver light that dawns upon my silent consciousness,
To terrify my soul with fate or gladden me with hope,
Add a guiding glimmer to the pathway of the messenger,
To draw a line demarking the dimensions of a dream;
Echoing across the tenuous expanse I hear the truth.

Hector de la O

66.

Fortune smiles on the few, the favored of the gods,
And they adapt themselves to an aberrant world,
Certain that they are no better than they who'd be so
Envious of them for that most highly-prized of gifts.

Lurking about in the shadow of those born to beauty
Is the vast majority, defaced by cruel destiny or birth,
Forced to face the knife of men who hide their fates
Thinking to compete with nature's finest work!

Héctor de la O – 17 JUL 02

67.

Men are born and forge their destinies and die,
In a world in which it had been better to have been
Cast as ne'er-do-wells, than to have as much success,
Histories sooner overshadowed by our later downfall,
And our only saving grace our talent, useless now,
Evoked by artificial memories conjured up by friends,
Loyal to the legacy we leave whose vestiges bring gain.

Jubilee awaits the diligent who've laid their riches up,
Attended to their tasks and banked their assets,
Careful not to turn to strangers with their earnings,
Knowing better than to buy beyond their humble means,
Secure in the integrity of one woman's love held fast,
Or the vanity which hides a man's true face prevails,
Nullifying our future in a world of our negated past.

Héctor de la O – 10 JUL 02

68.

Can I join your club that runs about like madmen,
Oblivious of the rage incited in the peaceful sleepers?
You wend your way about the silent neighborhood,
Often stopping to harangue us with your laughter;
To the fools the image of the docile in repose
Entertains the merrymakers and spurs them on to sport.

Forgive me if I trod your track with lead and fire,
Aiming as a slaver would to kill if not to maim.
My mind enlivened like the primal instincts in a dog,
I pine away for the perfume of a forbidden female,
Lurking in the dark to bring me fleeting pleasure;
You have no master but the moment you might waste.

Outside the wall you come and go without a hitch,
Unlike the rest of us who form the rank and file.
Truly free to savor liberty unhindered we could be,
If insistent conscience cancel its incessant censure.
Notwithstanding, can your mischief of the night before,
Greet the day that will not shade your deeds – unseen?

H. d. l. O – 17 OCT 08

69.

How can one be held accountable for innocence,
Unless you choose to call it being disingenuous?
My crimes against the state of grace these days,
All pale in their comparison to those egregious,
Nefarious acts of insolence so long ago atoned-for.

Blessed be les miserables for their hungry take,
Even those whose thirst to slake at foreign wells
Immerse them to be christened vile interlopers,
Not to mention any less a thief who robs a thief,
Gone wanting though his deeds envision gallantry.

Maybe David had no right to make Bathsheba his;
Enough had it have been to take another's wife,
And not another's right to life to hide a sin.
Never any less the light of mercy shone upon him,
So the gift of wisdom graced their son for love.

Besides all other crooked paths now straightened out,
Each by some Divine decree to sway us to compassion,
If by our own authority we need to likewise render
Niceties instead of vengeful retribution to each other,
God's perfection we have fallen short of to attain.

Heaven's witnesses look down upon us and our misdeeds,
Unaware of the pervasive nature of our passions' force.
Moreover can we anymore be comprehended from above,
As we are as terrestrial as any other animal,
Notwithstanding a spiritual nature rarely taken on.

H. d. l. O. (AUG '07 – JUL 08)

70.

Judge me for my illegitimate ethnicity,
Unable to accept me for my humble history.
And yet you pick my feeble brain for edifice,
Nibble at the words inside my skull tattooed.
Egotistical the bird of prey that stalks the mind,
Nibbling the flesh and bones of the unfortunates,
Independent never of the hunger for their truth,
Attesting but to knowing nothing of the origins,
So certain of the notions and ideas of others.

Picking nits like letters from a noodle soup,
Obtained from ordinary people never to recall,
Like the derelicts on Main Street their experience,
And still does art remain the envy of the intellect.
Never knowing more than what the head can store,
Can the musings of the thinkers rival serendipity,
Or however ancients sages' wisdom, words of babes?
I don't think so,
Do you?

Héctor de la O – 04 NOV 04

71.

Bin Laden has been all but now forgotten, unatoned,
Under Afghan skies so confident his hand onetime.
Saddam in his own land betrayed to strangers to despise,
Hailed up but with a pittance of the lucre he had known.

Sons are born to some whose strength succumbs to time;
Enough are taken in the lowborn streets, uncounted.
Now terrorist do fill the ranks so vacant heretofore,
To buckle on eternity so fleet to find by martyrdom.

Too soon a Texan hears his arms to repossess by force;
He could as easily have followed Don Corleone's lead,
Entreating Sunnidom to peace or enmity be flaunted;
Morning now, and emptiness pervades in many homes.

Also now the coffers cannot pay for the lost prestige abroad,
While the oil we already burned surpasses what we covet.
And acts of God lay siege to modern-day Gomorrahs,
You and I meanwhile attesting to apocalyptic history.

H. d. l. O – 21 AUG 07

Al Tikrit, your power to the gentiles changes hands.

72.

The fire will claim our sons and daughters!
How the children used to talk of fiery plans;
Every recess and the class would air one theme:
Death would come by flames instead of water.
In the interim before said holocaust I've seen
Rivers high above the coastline that no longer run,
Turning into instant floods to wash the hills away.
Instead of labor's fruits the weather should provide,
Summer seals the surface of the hardened clay.

Bearing witness now the daily necromancers weep,
Unlike the narcissistic pride they showed back then,
Receiving credit for the clemency the climate lent.
Never was lament for sunny days before thus heard,
If never either dancing for the rains of fall to come,
Not since our native brothers offered songs of hope,
Gainsaying the unabated fervor of this earthen crucible.
Until the burning rays of ire yield to autumn's rainfall,
Prevailing winds will fan the flames to bare the slopes.

H. d. l. O – 21 AUG 07

73.

Late in the life of my beloved homeland you appear,
And take no thought to leave us drowning in your debt;
My take on it is that you're here to alter destiny awhile,
Even as a blind man leaves his footprints unperceived.

Did you do your father's work or would he too deny you,
Until your followers most partisan have joined your foes.
Condescending to the kings, a lonely woman ill-at-ease,
Kinship to you entertains, intent on playing out her role.

But even your ambassadors belie your nefarious intent,
Unless a furrowed brow to anything but consternation
Should admit in their attempts to satisfy old doubts:
Humble though we seem we are all the more imperious.

Go headlong to your fate hell-bent to gain your library;
Of the Caesars' mettle but the dross of history remains.
Now these martyrs by divine decree invade our shores,
Emissaries of the eventuality of new eminent domains.

Héctor de la O – JAN 07

74.

Captive hearts were meant to learn to love,
And men would hope to win them in the end.
Rebelling from their choices could imperil you;
Meanwhile time and motherhood take hold,
Ensnaring with entertaining dreams of life,
Like the twinkling stars that carry us away,
In the morning bring us to the light to realize
That duty is the part of love that is our lot,
And we are pawns in someone else's game.

Gone the air of innocence we used to breathe,
On trial each day for crimes we never did commit,
To fill our souls our children's love we bought;
How dear the price but sweet the recompense.
Each one of us will someday be delivered whole,
Regardless of our age, and time were merciful.
When least you thought you'd ever see the day,
A God in Heaven saw your plight and rescued you.
Yet while your life was worth its liberty at least.

Hector de la O – 25 APR -5

Poor women, beaten into submission every day,
Somewhere in the world. I hope you get away.

75.

I came through here like a song without romance,
Like a lonely ghost without a change of ever being
Likely to be welcomed for the sake of my own love.
Born into an active world I couldn't call my own,
Effaced without a name that anyone respected,
Sojourner on the omnibus of morbid anonymity,
Ever here and never anywhere unto this very day.
Even so, I have my private microcosm to be sure;
I have no need of the mystique of strange associations.
Never taken but mistakenly absurd and still I was
Gregarious as a joyful man embracing his reflection.

Youth is gone but hope and joy remain the measure
Of my time with you and faith in a future yet to forge
Unseen surprises that we shouldn't fear to tempt.
Somehow we persist, negated efforts notwithstanding,
Of audacity emboldened in the face of unseen fallacy,
Modesty is never false in spirits that have failed them,
Either having fallen by the wayside for erroneous intent,
Through no doing of their own to fashion fate's finality.
If it be otherwise that destiny is authored by our hand,
May our time allotted be sufficient to defray the cost
Each wasted moment has delayed us in a lifetime lent.

Hector de la O –

76.

Do you want the master of the house to hear you.
Offering audible appreciation of the gustatory
Nature of your most recent sitting just enjoyed,
Today, like a child taking pride in making noise?

Burdening my ears with your gutteral enunciations,
Unduly, as if I'd welcome being privy to the menu!
Riotous staccato inviting me to some vicarious joy,
Partaking of your peptic interlude post-antipasto!

Lady now at table number two about to leave the room,
Ostentatious in her own right for her rattling gait,
Unabashedly usurping the silence of the sound waves,
Departs with the wind in her sails purveying pollution.

Hector de la O – AUG 09

77.

Gautama left the lap of luxury to suffer,
Among the mortals once ordained to die;
Until his great awakening no one told him
That even Suddhodana and Maha Maya could
Attempt for all their royal mien to hinder
Mara from his purpose to reclaim their son,
Although they would as lief prevent his mission.

Always mothers' sons and fathers' daughters free!
While to their detriment cold death should practice
Ambush after living without really living in a prison
Kinship and tradition oft inflict upon their offspring.
End result? In turn we thwart our children's lives,
Now by such endeavors to perpetuate the status quo,
So that complacency survives and mediocrity revives.

Hector de la O – JUN 02

78.

On my honor she's a lusty-looking wench!
Home life has to be the feeding of her snakes;
You could almost see her dancing if you fancied,
Or could summon up the images I offer you.
Look upon her smoothly-sinewed legs and weep!
As for me I'd pray they lock me in a scissors hold;
Never mind – She's brown as cinnamon to boot.
Did I mention that her rounded, sinewed calves
Are as worthy of insurance policies as Grable's?

Hector de la O – 27 JUN 02

Last time I saw her, she had changed - Private practice
And the good life took their toll – But I remember!

79.

\#1

Pomo princess plait your braids below the Badger's Pass,
Over by the lakes that trap the winter's whispers.
Raise your cup and toast the harvest amaranth
Cyclical springtimes once and ever since have offered you.
In deference to the beauty of your belly like a platter,
Undulating under native suns your golden wild oats.
Now reach out with your left hand – Nurture me;
Collect for me the prickly pears and piñón nuts and point
Unto the waters with your right hand where you hide the sun.
Late into the night we sing and dance to honor you,
And the child deep withing our spirits calls you Mother.

Héctor de la O – 06.25.02

El Pueblo de Nuestra Señora,
Le Reina de Los Angeles de Porciúncula
(The old)

80.

\#2

Put in modern terms we waive the right to claim you,
Our Matriarch whose heart has turned to stone.
Right your craft before you wreck along the shore;
Celebrity precedes you yet celerity deceives you,
In a town where fleet longevity will leave you prone
Unfailingly to make-up and the strip mall liquor store.
No one knows where we have lost you when night falls,
Clunking like a hub cap as it bounces to the curb.
Unlike other children in whose mother rest assured,
Late at night you leave us praying for the peaceful dawn,
And at daybreak blinded by our tears we hear the door.
06.26.02

El Pueblo de Nuestra Señora,
La Reina de Los Angeles de Porciúncula
(The new)

81.

Put your pen to paper and the ink will never flow –
Oh, what's the good of endless pages to an empty soul?
Each another trading dog-eared verses thrice unfurled,
To café bards and lyricists encumbering the world.
So, what to say to innocents desisting not to crave
Ability to strum the strings and an agility to phrase?
Read until your eyes close and decry the failing love,
Earthly though it be or it be given from above.

Inspired as we feel we are, nobody knows by whom,
Not a one of us will hold his peace though doomed
So cruelly to hear the empty phrasing of our words.
Put a price on any song you think the Spirit's urged;
In a word stand firm if you have found your voice.
Regardless of the consequences of a dubious choice,
Everyone who rides the rhythm of the muse's mare,
Departs astride his madness, his peculiar pain to bare.

Héctor de la O – 21 JUN 02

82.

Once you told me were "long in the tooth"
However you were young and lovely as today.
Could I boldly ask you now to look upon me then
As something other than the lowly man you see?
Right it is though it could ever be as you perceive.
Lay your weapons down as I'm no harm to you,
And all I ask is that you truly be a friend to me.

May I inquire now as to your feminine prerogative?
And couldn't womankind be just as Juliet described.
Unable for the lunacy their constant word to give?
Rely on mine for truth is stable as a yearning soul:
Each day I was away and cannot fathom why,
Evocative in thought and dreams you came to me;
No other woman held a habitation in my heart.

H. d. l. O – 12 OCT 11

83.

What if all the universal elements comingle,
And then melt with no human form resulting?
Instead of sloth you should diligence employ,
To do my paperwork before the Second Coming.

Single out the least of these petitioners anon,
Or if with empathy you dealt with all of us,
Municipal or County Service could enjoy
Eulogies instead of epithets so well-deserved.

Meanwhile don't we dread you minions more,
Ordained as we all are, to suffer time's sufficiency,
Relegated to be seen by you a nuisance and a chore,
Even as our own thoughts aim beyond the window?

Hector de la O –

84.

Bonehead bending all the rules to make it plain:
Of all the morons east & west & north & south,
May God have mercy on your mindless soul!
But how you find the beaten path again,
And never stray so far your foot can't find
So sure its way back into your mouth who knows?
The nature of the beast is to empower the image
It portrays, not so unlike an ancient river's flow
Celerity displays, and never ceases to deliver all
Its water to the sea – and not a drop returns.
Thus it's written that the tongue will never budge,
Yet its helmsman shall be judged for every idle word.

Héctor de la O –

85.

Today will be the first day of the final years,
Hoping against hope I don't get Jacob's lot;
It would be another four for Rachel's hand,
So I pray for all the patience of the patriarchs.
And we can see the horsemen's dust already,
Looking skyward all the spirits of the faithful,
Like we also see the faintest flicker of the fires,
Begging for the winds of time to fan the flames.
Each day I'll also pray my trials have atoned;
Germane to this interminable exile is my folly.
All the charm of these exotic lands could hold me
Not a second more nor keep me for a second time.

Judge me anyway but able to forget my home,
Unless unworthy of another miracle I thus remain,
Suspended in a fateful interlude by cruel destiny,
Tangled in this temporal maze of worldly cares,
Like so many common men defiled by their greed.
In truth I'd sell all that I own and give it to the poor,
Knowing I'm as homeless and as penniless as they;
Evil I appear and pale by comparison to them.
Tomorrow shall I share a table with my very own;
Hector shall be saved this time from accursed giants,
If my mainsail billowed by an unseen breeze of mercy
Send me home again to there await the Armageddon.

Héctor de la O – 16 AUG 04

86.

Give me not that which to fear of fate,
Or the condemnation of a wayward son,
Devout before You, but in absence,
Hiding from the Light though You remain,
As near as every breath, Your essence,
Veiled by our denials, diaphanous and dark,
Effervescing like excuses on the Final Day.

Many times have I offended You with folly;
Every time again You prove a father's love,
Reminding me that I in faith should rise above
Civility alone and never wander more in deed.
You save me from my sin although it still be hot,
Or from a heartless soul, its cold as of a tomb,
No heart for You there found, awaiting death.

So now I pray not only for myself but for us all,
In life or in the grave to know that we are Yours;
No place to hide for Godless, unrepentant men,
Nor errant children, forever gone astray from truth.
Each one of us who seeks Your way with deepest care,
Relies upon Your promises as I abide in joy and peace,
Secure in every step I take when I Your counsel heed.

H. d. I. O – 02 NOV 07

My daughter, Asia, turns 36 today!

87.

Have you ever done unto another so unlike a lover,
In a manner you would never have expected of her?
So, you thought you were above her and that you also
Governed her vicissitudes innate and a hormonal sway?
Obligation stifled, soon nefarious instincts will abound,
Often in the hearts of slighted women unrestrained.
So, all the imperfections of our race are to be found,
Ever present just beneath the surface in the tame.

If a woman's kindness, sleeping with an enemy can cease,
So provoked of tenderness gone lacking and treachery,
Can you keep her from her vengeance on a peaceful day?
Or if another love her in your absence to your detriment,
On what principle can you be blameless for her perfidies?
Knowing your philandering can make a goodly woman turn
Even into the most salacious strumpet though you had her heart,
Do then play at anything but love duplicitous so prone to burn.

H. d. I. O – 19 FEB '08

88.

Living in a land you cannot hope to own,
And suffering from woes you less deserve –
Unlike the harmful people who have shown
Reproach for you – but dare you ever swerve,
And then all hope is lost to end your days alone.

Lend an ear to Heaven's truth now voiced:
In Jesus' mercy you have ever dwelt –
Not one has never made some wrongful choice,
Designed to end in all the pain we felt,
And who has loved without a heart is less adroit.

Maintain that joy of yours and do not be dismayed,
And keep your faith so you can win the prize
Reserved for all the children worthy by the grace,
In Jesus's Holy Name for each of us devised,
As well as on this earth to find our place.

Lend now an ear to him whose eyes have seen
A woman beautiful and gracious all her life,
Undone by illness and abandonment – a queen
Remaining 'til the end though you were not a wife;
All things work for your own good if you have Faith.

H. d. I. O – 30 SEP 02

89.

Alarms are tripped in hearts so prone to strife;
Lent to their arms their brazen pennants soar,
To wage their war against a populace at peace,
As he whom Abraham once blessed is wont to do.
Get thee hence from such if kinship should endure,
Restrained from crossing sabers 'til the calm return
And bring all Temuchins their case to rest at last,
Cessation of discord to reunite a family in the end.
If guile not cast a shadow on the truth and honesty
Availed of generosity sustain your seed as if at all.

90.

Ever wonder who they are whom we detest?
Vile lackeys of a system that empowers them;
If to have said power is to be like God Himself,
Let them learn of the corruption of the flesh.

Relegate me to removal like the refuse that I am;
Equality with usurpers of the very judgment seat
Never let me in my brightest dreams desire attain,
Even as the angels they of false investiture once did,
Eh?

Go then to the farthest reaches of unwelcome forums;
Onerous your very presence and you cackle like a hen!
Now the judge, that simple little man will come to learn
Every deed you perpetrated under color of authority.

And may wisdom teach us thus to hear the minions
Who have lorded over us a little less as time elapses,
As of a surety a your temporal estate will come asunder;
Yet shall you ill repent but fall for hollow pride instead.

H. d. l. O – 04 DEC 08

91.

Valentine

Be mine,
As I am yours,
And as he was to her
And shall be for always.

He lived
A time with her,
A prisoner for love,
And then he went the way.

His love
He proffered her,
And love she learned from him,
When love was hard to learn.

I'd love
To love you now,
Just as he loved her then,
As innocent and pure.

One day,
They brought him there
To languish for a while,
And thus await his fate.

But love
Sustained him there,
And so he languished not,
For fairly flew the days.

Now you,
So far away
From everything you know,
Can know I love you still.

And I,
Though I'm alone
Between my life and death,
Am succored by your love.

Alone,
But not alone,
The paradox of love:
In love we're not alone.

One day
We shall be gone,
And never shall return
To love beneath this sun.

He too,
When time was up,
Was lain upon the block,
Or given to the lions

For now,
While I can love,
I'll do as he once did,
Whose name was Valentine.

Héctor de la O – FEB 90

92.

Lost forever is my place in an old Utopian world
Of girls in heels and miniskirts with pleats awhirl,
Sometime before the advent of pantyhose and discos.
All the magic has gone underground to begin marking
Nether-time in darkened downtown warehouses,
Gyrating in a feverish press of poisoned bodies,
Every dancer's passions fueled by fatal ecstasy.
Love-ins happened in flowery meadows in the sun;
Eventide now glowers at the offspring of the night,
Sullen shadows only of the children as they were.

Héctor de la O – 26 FEB 02

93.

In the Land of Plenty did they ply their trade,
Native speakers and the language of the law,
Talking while the talkers themselves talked,
Every word they spoke and nothing less,
Rapid as a fully-automatic bead of sweat,
Panting after every thought they uttered,
Righteous in the knowledge of the lexicon
Exploding through the mental threshold,
Thundering through the air like foreign birds,
Electric as the light of syllables they heard,
Regarded as the speakers of the golden truth,
So swift they couldn't think before the word.

And if their eyes devoid of tears could weep,
Rebel indeed against the perpetuity of lies,
Every man or woman by the dock would cry,
Alarmed at this audacity of stubborn advocates,
Pugnacious in the face of irrefutable facts.
And they were anything but speechless on the fly,
That is if terms of art were not elusive creatures
Harbored in some hearts, too fearful to emerge.
Eventually their phrases raced with a rapacity
Too resonant to trail behind like shadows
In the footsteps of their authors, like echoes;
Cautious never, but impulsive as an instant urge.

H. d. l. O – 08 SEP 04

94.

Mescalito happened by while we were visiting
Eden's outskirts with our Indian-looking ladies,
X-raying each others' souls so Kreskinesquely.
I felt the presence of the Guardian at my side.
Can you imagine climbing into someone else's soul?
Allies of the Master lingered at the morrow's door,
Nurturing the energy that vaults the firmament
Of stars like neon freckles on the cobalt canopy;
Nestled meanwhile we below upon the desert floor.

My every fiber could ignore the evil on the Earth,
Enveloped as I was in the embrace of nascent calm,
Serene this voyager by place and time unhindered,
Captained by the conscious essence of the succulents.
And the evildoers ridiculed me from the riverbed,
Like a coven of coyotes howling mirthfully at me.
In the morning allies of the night before convened,
Neighborly confiding their complaints of travesties,
Eclipsing yesterday's event of equine evil I restrained.

My friend Mario Inclán once quieted barking dogs,
Ordering them to silence with an unuttered word.
Reservations hinder natives, not so bodhisattvas
Emerging from their slumber in colorblind environs,
Propelled into the Presence of the Power of the air,
Or so It's called, Which has dominion over Nature.
Which is better, knowledge of the world, or wisdom?
Every member of our race can have them both.
Regard the former temporal; the latter is Eternal.

Héctor de la O – 12 AUG 04

About the Author

The author began using the professional name Héctor de la O in
the entertainment community in 1980, working as an engineer for
a local radio station in Woodburn, Oregon – It is a surname of his
maternal great-grandmother. Beginning around that time, Hector
became a member of two well-known Latin American folklore bands
in the Northwest, (first Antara, and then Grupo Kultura) playing
the Seattle Folk Life Festival for several years as well as many local
venues and events, from the Portland area, to all points around
Oregon and Washington.

Hector was born in a Mexican-American family in Los Angeles,
California, where he was raised – graduated from Wilson High
School of El Sereno, California in 1966, when he joined the
Marines - After a three-year stint which included duty in Viet Nam,
he went to several colleges, including East L.A., Cal State L.A.,
Sweetwater and Western Oregon University, majoring in Language
arts, receiving two degrees.

I already knew Hector as a linguist and creative spirit who spent his
down-time at his sinecure in the courthouse attached to the Men's
Central Jail on Bauchet Street, drawing, writing and adding to the
Aztlán Chicano art altar on his desk, a collage of symbols, pictures
and objects (an eternal work-in-progress that expressed the subtleties
of his soul).

He also spoke poetry, a language above the laws of grammar and
syntax and the every-day manner we are accustomed to, of making
connection with, and expressing what we see and feel. His "verses",
as he calls them, remind me of a braid of dreams, a flow of thought
that exist beyond the linear logic. These writings, like some stylized

chronicle, entwine his boyhood in Northeast Los Angeles with his experience as a warrior in Viet Nam, and then again with his love of the beaty of the barrio world – all evident in a wisdom that is hard-won by holding fast to hope and love and all that is tender, in spite of the knowledge of violence and decay and inevitable loss – aware that this game is rigged.

As I read these poems on late afternoons, on my balcony overlooking the palm trees and apartment building rooftops, realizing the horizon moves toward the sunsets of an ocean I can't see from here, I wondered if there was some hidden meaning in all I was reading – I did ask the author, who answered cryptically, "Could be." This is a compilation of an observer's experience with the spectacle of life, joy and suffering, offered to us in a multi-colored spiritual kaleidoscope.

Hector lives in the Northwest to this date, and is semi-retired as a Court-certified interpreter for several states and the U.S. Federal Court. Since only his associates in the entertainment realm know him by his nom de plume, good luck finding him. Hector does welcome your communication, and sends his greetings to anyone who might read his thoughts (or whose thoughts he may have read). I invite you all to experience what I did in these astonishing pieces.
Robert Rammelkamp [O.H.P.]